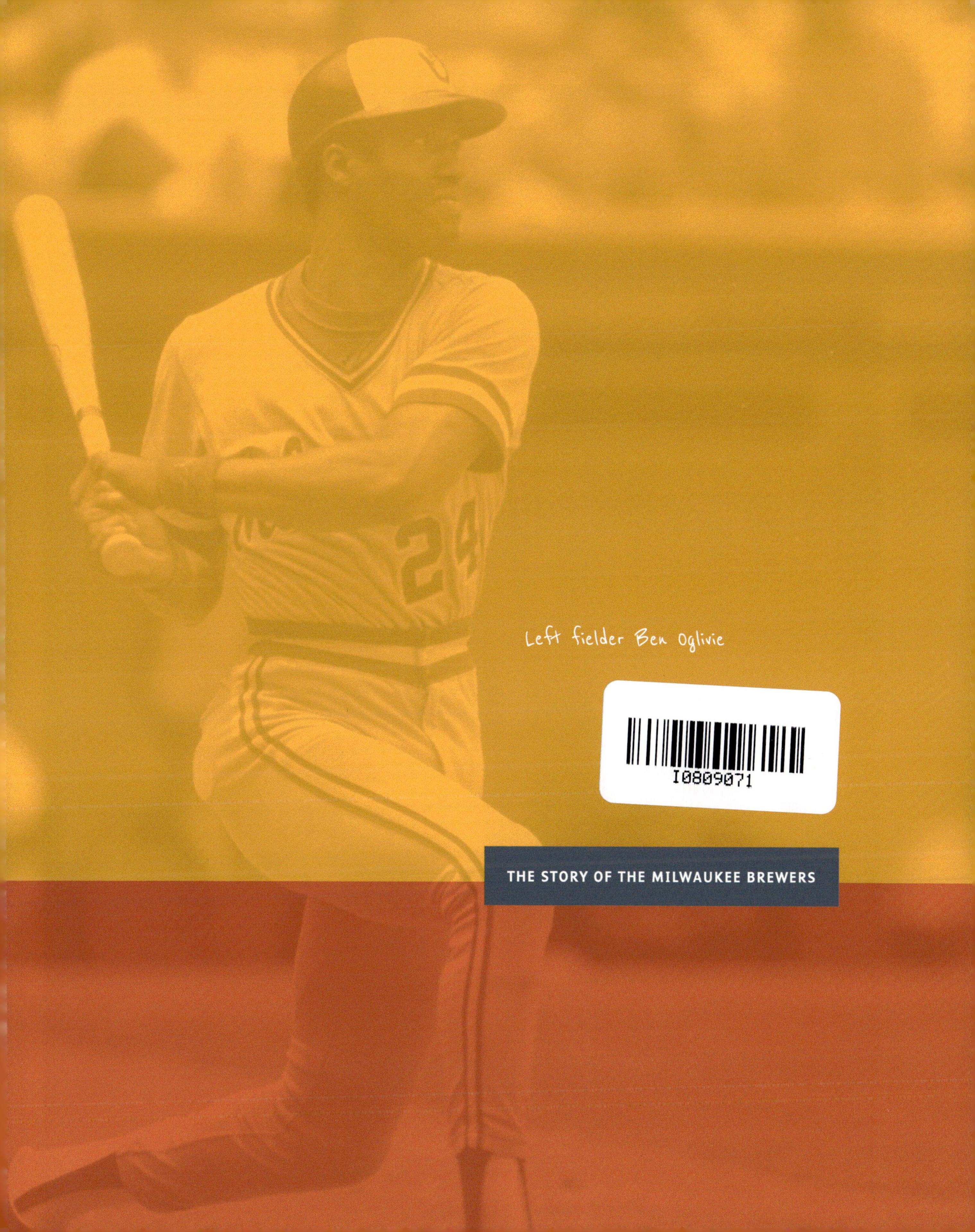

Left fielder Ben Oglivie

THE STORY OF THE MILWAUKEE BREWERS

Outfielder Jackson Chourio

THE STORY OF THE

MILWAUKEE BREWERS

JOE TISCHLER

Left fielder Christian Yelich

CREATIVE SPORTS

CREATIVE EDUCATION / CREATIVE PAPERBACKS

Published by Creative Education and Creative Paperbacks
P.O. Box 227, Mankato, Minnesota 56002
Creative Education and Creative Paperbacks are imprints of
The Creative Company
www.thecreativecompany.us

Book Design by Graham Morgan
Art direction by Blue Design (www.bluedes.com)

Images by Alamy Stock Photo/Cal Sport Media, 3; Associated Press/Jeffrey Phelps, cover; Getty Images/Bill Smith, 10, Brad Mangin, 23, Bruce Kluckhohn, 24–25, Erick W. Rasco, 2, Focus On Sport, 7 (top, left), 7 (top, right), George Kubas/Diamond Images, 28–29, 31, Jonathan Daniel, 19, Otto Greule Jr, cover, 10, 18, Rich Pilling, 1, 4–5, 6 (top, right), 6 (bottom, left), 7 (bottom, right), 15, 20, 32, Rob Tringali, 30, Ron Vesely, 9, Ronald C. Modra, 16, Scott Boehm, 6 (bottom, right), Scott Wachter/Time Life Pictures, 6 (top, left), Tom Lynn, 7 (bottom, left), 11; Public Domain/12; Wikimedia Commons/Spaluch1, 27

Library of Congress Cataloging-in-Publication Data
Names: Tischler, Joe author
Title: The story of the Milwaukee Brewers / by Joe Tischler.
Description: Mankato, Minnesota : Creative Education and Creative Paperbacks, [2026] | Series: Creative sports. Major League baseball | Includes index. | Audience: Ages 8-12 | Audience: Grades 4-6 | Summary: "Discover the Milwaukee Brewers' thrilling journey from dramatic playoff runs to recent successes, featuring legendary players, iconic moments, and the Major League Baseball team's enduring resilience and determination Written for middle-grade readers. Includes table of contents, sidebars, and index"– Provided by publisher.
Identifiers: LCCN 2025020676 (print) | LCCN 2025020677 (ebook) | ISBN 9798895810996 library binding | ISBN 9798896800521 paperback | ISBN 9798895812259 ebook
Subjects: LCSH: Milwaukee Brewers (Baseball team)–History–Juvenile literature. | Baseball–Wisconsin–Milwaukee–History, Local–Juvenile literature.
Classification: LCC GV875.M53 T57 2026 (print) | LCC GV875.M53 (ebook) | DDC 796.357/640977594–dc23/eng/20250621
LC record available at https://lccn.loc.gov/2025020676
LC ebook record available at https://lccn.loc.gov/2025020677

Printed in the United States

Center fielder Gorman Thomas

34

15

Brewers
23

CONTENTS

EXTRA INNINGS

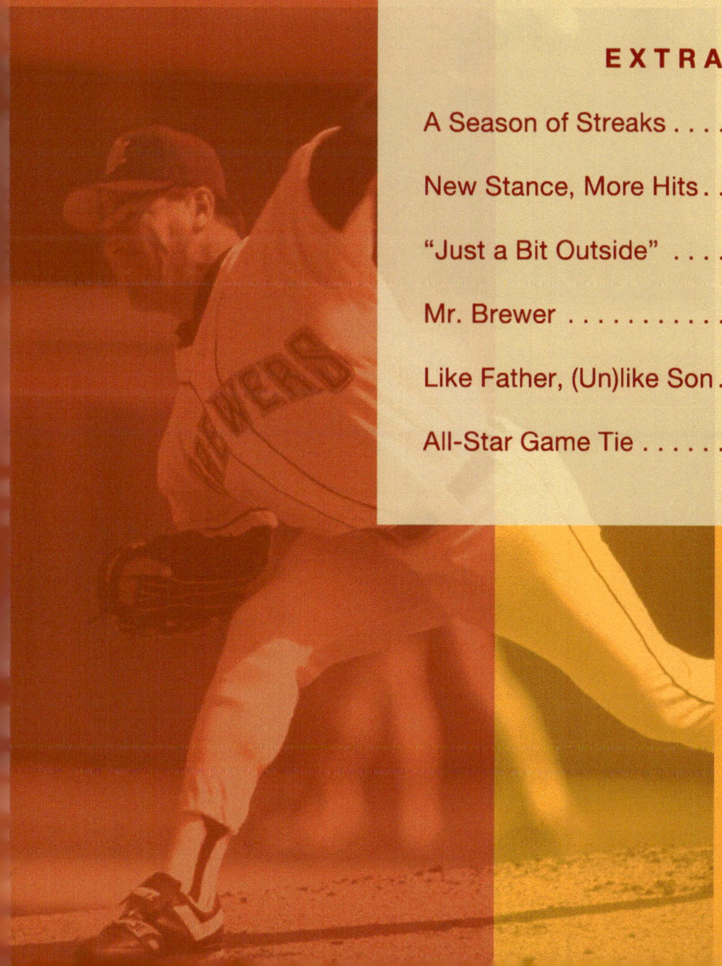

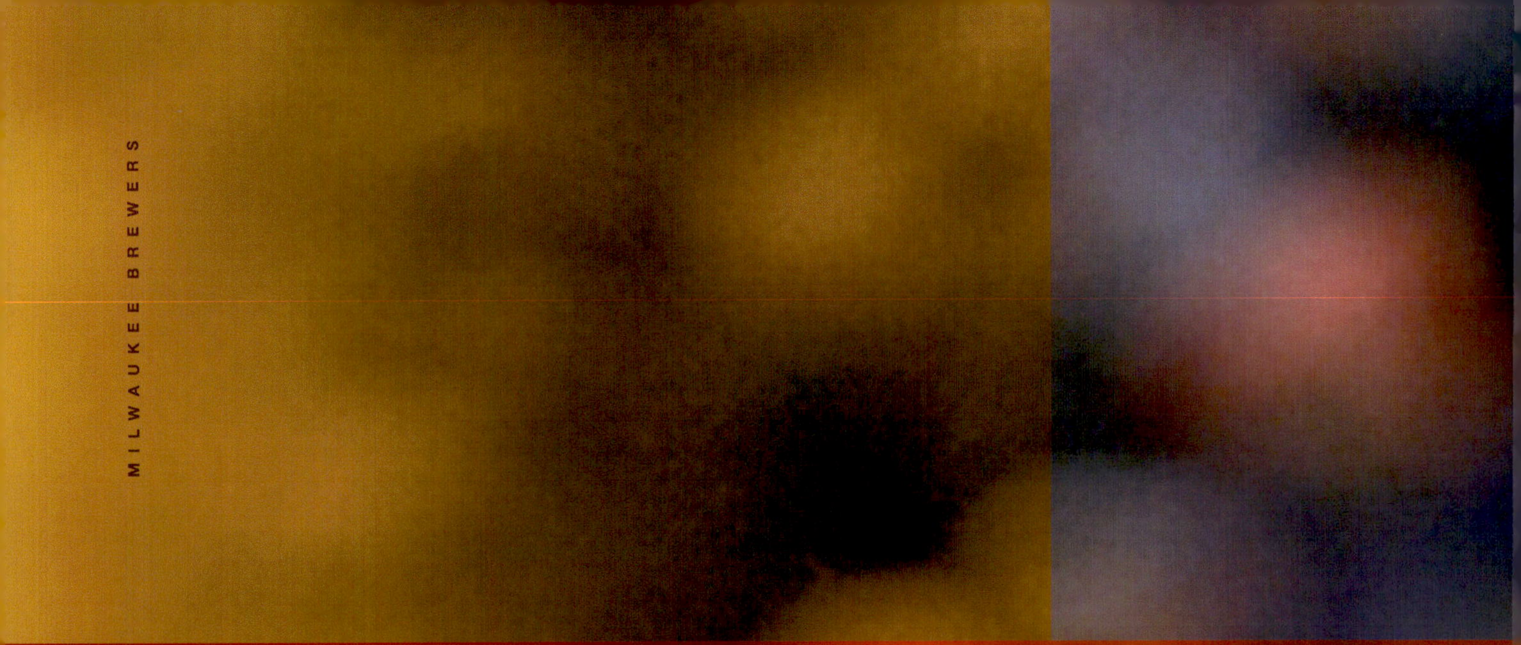

CHASING JOE

One of Major League Baseball's (MLB) most recognizable streaks is that of Joe DiMaggio. In 1941, the former New York Yankees slugger had a hit in 56 straight games. Since then, Pete Rose of the Cincinnati Reds came closest to equaling the feat. In 1978, he had a 44-game hitting streak. In 1987, Paul Molitor of the Milwaukee Brewers did his best to reach Rose and maybe even DiMaggio.

Molitor had a good, yet frustrating, start to the 1987 season. The third baseman missed 43 games because of injury through the first three months of the season. When healthy, he batted .323. On July 16, Molitor was back from a 16-game absence. He started the game at designated hitter. He had one hit in four at-bats against the California Angels. It was not much. But it was the start of a streak. The next day, he had three hits. In a four-game home series against the Oakland Athletics, Molitor had two three-hit games. Those included the first home runs of the hit streak, which now stood at 10. By the end of July, the hit streak was at 15 games. Molitor's batting average rose to .350.

Third baseman Paul Molitor

EXTRA INNINGS

Infielder Paul Molitor

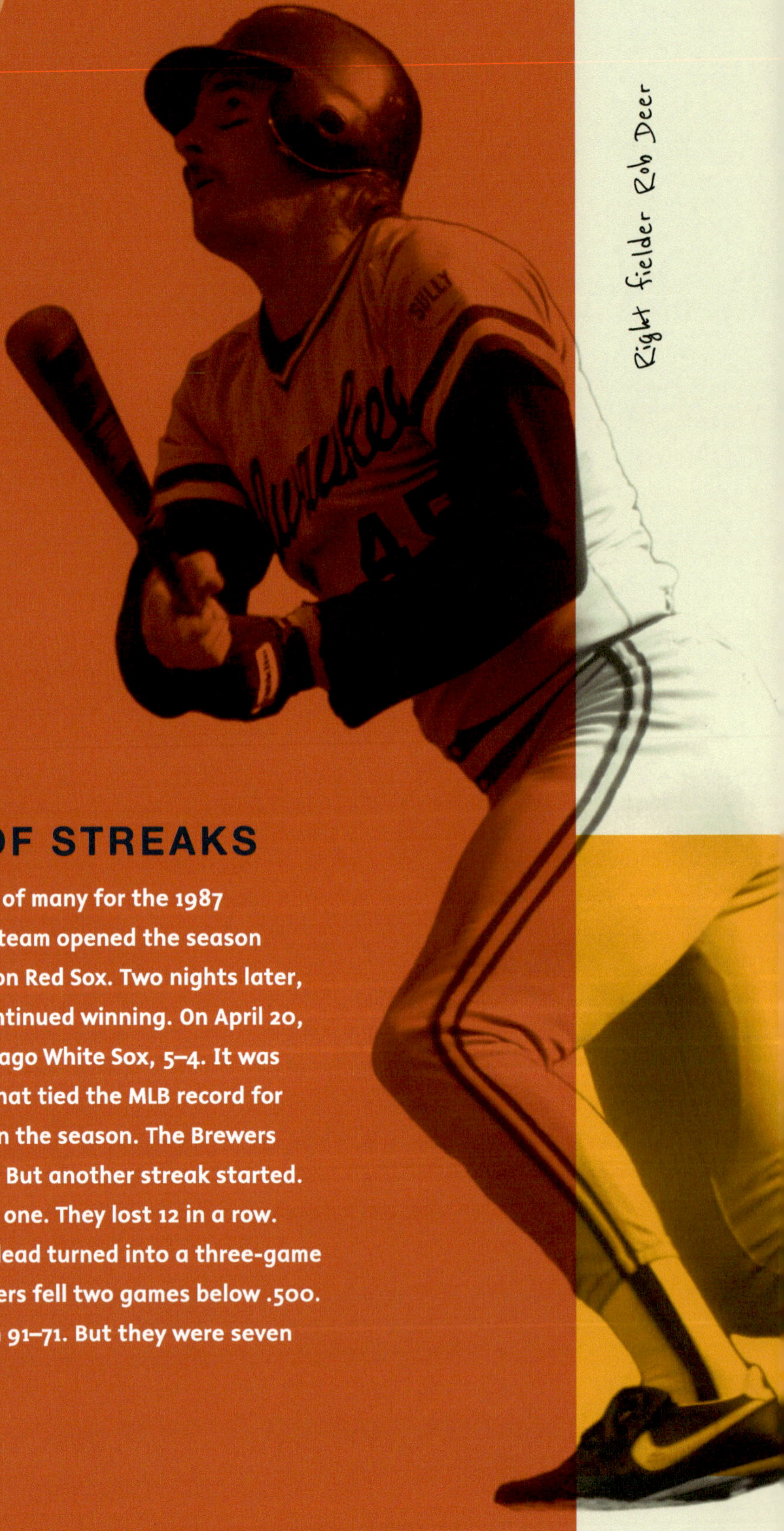

Right fielder Rob Deer

A SEASON OF STREAKS

Molitor's streak was one of many for the 1987 Milwaukee Brewers. The team opened the season with a win over the Boston Red Sox. Two nights later, they won again. They continued winning. On April 20, Milwaukee beat the Chicago White Sox, 5–4. It was their 13th win in a row. That tied the MLB record for consecutive wins to begin the season. The Brewers started the season 20–3. But another streak started. This time, it was a losing one. They lost 12 in a row. Their five-game division lead turned into a three-game deficit. In July, the Brewers fell two games below .500. They rebounded to finish 91–71. But they were seven games out of first place.

Pitcher Teddy Higuera

August started with multi-hit games in two of the Brewers five games. In a three-game series against the Texas Rangers, Molitor went 8-for-12 to extend the streak to 27. Three one-hit games followed. The streak reached 30. Fans started to realize the kind of roll Molitor was on.

Molitor had his first four-hit game of the streak against the Cleveland Indians. That was part of a four-game series where he had 10 hits in 20 at-bats. The hitting streak was now at 35 games. Hits in four more games followed.

On August 26, the hitting streak was at 39. Molitor played as designated hitter throughout the streak. His batting average during the streak was .415. His season average rose to .370. The Brewers hosted Cleveland on this day. Teddy Higuera was pitching for Milwaukee. John Farrell was the starter for Cleveland. Hits were hard to come by for both teams. Through nine innings, the game was scoreless. Both pitchers allowed only three hits each. Molitor was hitless in his first three at-bats. In the eighth inning, he reached base on an error. In the bottom of the 10th inning, the Brewers had runners on first and second with one out. Rick Manning was the pinch hitter. Molitor was the on-deck batter. Fans were eagerly waiting for him to extend the hitting streak to 40. But he didn't get the chance. Manning hit a single up the middle

Bob Hazle
OUTFIELD MILWAUKEE BRAVES
Red Schoendienst
2nd BASE MILWAUKEE BRAVES
Andy Pafk
OUTFIELD MILWAUKEE BRA
Ernie Johnson
PITCHER MILWAUKEE BRAVES
Warren Spahn
PITCHER MILWAUKEE BRAVES
Gene Conle
PITCHER MILWAUKEE BR
Joe Adcock
1st BASE MILWAUKEE BRAVES
Del Rice
CATCHER MILWAUKEE BRAVES
Don McMaho
PITCHER MILWAUKEE BRA

to allow Mike Felder to score the winning run. Instead of fans cheering for the win, Manning was met with boos from the home Milwaukee crowd. "Poor Rick Manning. He gets the winning hit and all of a sudden he's a bum," said Brewers center fielder Robin Yount.

Molitor's 39-game hitting streak is seventh-longest in MLB history. "To have the support of teammates and the fan reaction throughout the streak is something I'll always remember," said Molitor.

BREWING BASEBALL

Prior to the season of streaks, baseball had a long tradition in Milwaukee, Wisconsin. The city's first MLB team started in 1901. They were known as the Brewers. They lasted only one year before moving to St. Louis, Missouri. They are now the Baltimore Orioles. The city also hosted a successful minor-league team from 1902 to 1952. It was also named the Brewers. The name paid tribute to another Milwaukee tradition: brewing beer.

In 1953, MLB baseball returned to Milwaukee. The Boston Braves moved to the city. In their first season, the Braves set a major-league record for attendance. Nearly two million fans went to games throughout the season. The team won the 1957 World Series. In 1962, a new group of owners wanted to move the team to Atlanta, Georgia. There were no MLB teams in the southern United States. The television market was far greater there. The Braves moved after the 1965 season. Baseball returned to Milwaukee five years later. Bud Selig acquired the Seattle Pilots. They were an expansion team

Milwaukee Braves baseball cards

the year prior. He moved the team to Milwaukee just before the 1970 season and renamed the team Brewers.

The new Brewers suffered losing records during their first eight seasons in Milwaukee. One of the few highlights was first baseman George Scott. He won the Gold Glove award in all five seasons he was with the team.

In 1978, the Brewers finally had their first winning season. Their 93–69 finish earned them third place in the American League (AL) East Division. The team had some great players. Cecil Cooper covered first base. Rookie sensation Paul Molitor manned second. Curly-haired Robin Yount played shortstop. He had joined the team in 1974 at the age of 18. "We could all feel it," Yount said later. "We knew we were getting better. We knew that the pieces were fitting into place."

Milwaukee started the 1979 season stocked with sluggers, from Cooper to center fielder Gorman Thomas. Its lineup was packed with power. The team led the AL East with 185 home runs. But it finished the season second in its division. The Brewers racked up a league-leading 203 home runs the following season. They had to settle for third in the AL East.

A players' strike in 1981 brought play to a halt in June. Once games resumed, Milwaukee gained the best record in the season's second half. That qualified them for the playoffs for the first time. Milwaukee faced the New York Yankees in the AL Division Series (ALDS). New York won the first two games. The Brewers took the next two. In the deciding Game 5, the Brewers took an early lead. But the Yankees won the game and the series.

The team totaled 216 home runs in 1982. Yount led the league in several offensive categories. He was named AL Most Valuable Player (MVP) and won Gold Glove and Silver Slugger awards. The Brewers won the AL East. They faced the California Angels in the AL Championship Series (ALCS). Milwaukee lost the first two games on the road. But it rebounded to win the next three at home and claim the pennant.

EXTRA INNINGS

CECIL COOPER
FIRST BASEMAN
BREWERS SEASONS: 1977–87
HEIGHT: 6-FOOT-2
WEIGHT: 165 POUNDS
KEY STATS: 5X ALL-STAR, 2X GOLD GLOVE, 3X SILVER SLUGGER, 2X AL RBI LEADER

NEW STANCE, MORE HITS

Cecil Cooper began his MLB career with the Boston Red Sox. He hit a respectable .283 over six seasons with the team. Cooper was traded to the Brewers in 1977. Before the season, he changed his batting stance to resemble that of Rod Carew. Carew had won multiple batting titles with the Minnesota Twins. He would bat leaning far back on his left foot with his arms extended. The new stance helped Cooper. He hit .300 in his first season with the Brewers. Six more seasons with averages of .300 or higher followed. These included a career-high .352 average in 1980. Cooper's biggest hit came in 1982. In Game 5 of the ALCS, the Brewers trailed 3–2 in the seventh inning. With two outs and the bases loaded, Cooper delivered a single to left field that scored two. The Brewers won 4–3. They reached the World Series for the first time.

EXTRA INNINGS

BOB UECKER
BREWERS BROADCASTER
1971–2024

"JUST A BIT OUTSIDE"

Bob Uecker played nearly 300 games over six MLB seasons. He gained his fame after his playing career. He began his broadcasting career with his hometown Milwaukee Brewers in 1971. He continued to be the main play-by-play radio voice of the team through the 2024 season. Uecker earned the nickname of "Mr. Baseball." He was well known for his comedic persona. He appeared often on *The Tonight Show with Johnny Carson*. He was a regular on the 1980s sitcom *Mr. Belvedere*. Uecker also appeared in the *Major League* movie franchise. He played Harry Doyle, broadcaster for the Cleveland Indians. His catch phrase from the movie was "just a bit outside" in reference to a pitch that was well outside of the strike zone. Uecker passed away just shy of his 91st birthday, shortly before the 2025 season.

Milwaukee met the St. Louis Cardinals in the World Series. It won Game 1 by 10 runs. The Cardinals took the next two games. The Brewers won Games 4 and 5. Then St. Louis rolled to a 13–1 victory in Game 6. The Cardinals won the deciding game.

POSTSEASON DROUGHT

Fans showed support following the Brewers' World Series appearance. A franchise-record 2,397,131 people jammed into Milwaukee County Stadium over the 1983 season. But they could not cheer the team into the playoffs. It was the start of one of the longest playoff droughts in professional sports history. The team would endure 25 years without an appearance in the postseason.

The power of Milwaukee's lineup was either gone or aging by 1984. The team finished the season 67–94. Only two years after their World Series appearance, the Brewers had fallen to the bottom of the division. In 1985, hard-throwing rookie pitcher Teddy Higuera gave the team hope. He tallied 15 wins. He won 20 the following season. But his teammates struggled at the plate. Milwaukee finished sixth in the division both years.

The Brewers charged out of the gate in 1987. Young southpaw Juan Nieves threw a no-hitter on April 15. By the end of the month, the Brewers had a remarkable 18–3 record. They went on to win 91 games. But they finished third in the AL East. The team came in third again the following year. Paul Molitor, Robin Yount, and catcher B. J. Surhoff gave solid offensive performances. But the Brewers kept posting disappointing records.

Infielder B. J. Surhoff

Things picked up again in 1992. Pitchers Chris Bosio and Cal Eldred each put together 10-game winning streaks. The team stole a league-leading 256 bases. Rookie shortstop Pat Listach accounted for a franchise-record 54 of those. He won AL Rookie of the Year honors. Milwaukee rallied for a 92–70 finish. It narrowly missed the playoffs. In 1993, they tumbled to 69–93. They were last in the AL East. Molitor left. Yount retired.

MLB switched to a three-division setup in 1994. Milwaukee finished last in the newly formed AL Central Division. Like the team itself, the Brewers' longtime ballpark, County Stadium, had seen better days. The state of Wisconsin approved financing for a new home field.

The Brewers started strong in 1995. They were within a half-game of the Wild Card by the end of August. But they faded in September. Milwaukee finished fourth in the AL Central. The following year, the Brewers finished out of playoff contention again. Slugging right fielder Jeromy Burnitz gave fans hope in 1997. He hit 27 home runs in his first full year as a starter. But the playoff drought continued.

Right fielder Jeromy Burnitz

EXTRA INNINGS

ROBIN YOUNT
SHORTSTOP/CENTER FIELDER
BREWERS SEASONS: 1974–93
HEIGHT: 6-FOOT-0
WEIGHT: 165 POUNDS
KEY STATS: 1999 HALL OF FAME INDUCTEE, 2X AL MVP, 3X ALL-STAR, 3X SILVER SLUGGER

MR. BREWER

Robin Yount was an outstanding all-around player. He had solid defensive skills and a strong stroke at the plate. Yount joined the 3,000-hit club in 1992. He later became the first Brewers player elected to the Hall of Fame. He was also appreciated for his loyalty to the team. He spent his entire 20-year career in Milwaukee. Teammate Gorman Thomas called Yount the best player he had ever seen. "He went full out all the time," said Thomas. "He might not have been the best hitter or the best shortstop or the best whatever. But he was the best player." Yount won two AL MVP awards at two different positions. In 1982 he played shortstop. In 1989, he played center field.

SHIFTING LEAGUES

MLB added two expansion teams in 1998. The Arizona Diamondbacks would play in the NL. The Tampa Bay Devil Rays would join the AL. Each league would then have 15 teams. But the odd number would pose major scheduling challenges. To solve the problem, the Brewers moved to the NL. That way each league had an even number of teams. Milwaukee joined the NL Central Division. In 1998, it won only 74 games. The results of the next two seasons were similar.

Fans hoped the new ballpark would bring a better future. Miller Park opened on April 6, 2001. The Brewers swept the first series in their new home stadium. "I believe there's a lot of exciting days and nights ahead for many, many years at Miller Park," said manager Davey Lopes after the series. "I think the anticipation, the excitement, matched everything that everybody expected it to be, and maybe even more."

That excitement continued to build throughout the first half of the season. First baseman Richie Sexson, left fielder Geoff Jenkins, and Burnitz displayed powerful hitting. The team hit 209 home runs. All those big swings had a downside, though. Milwaukee batters struck out 1,399 times. It was the highest in MLB that season. Milwaukee fizzled to a fourth-place finish in the NL Central.

In 2002, the Brewers lost 12 of their first 15 games. It was the worst start in team history. Milwaukee finished with just 56 wins. Outfielder Scott Podsednik had a great rookie season the following year. He batted .314 and stole 43 bases. Sexson belted 45 home runs. They improved to 68 wins. Sexson was then traded.

The trade brought in six new players. One was first baseman Lyle Overbay. He led the team with a .301 average in 2004. Another was catcher Chad Moeller. In April, he hit for the cycle (a single, double, triple, and home run in the same game). Milwaukee was above the .500 mark at the All-Star break. Then the team's bats fell silent. It finished last again.

The Brewers continued to miss the playoffs. But there were signs of hope. In an April 2006 game, five players hit home runs in a single inning. That tied a major-league record. Among those hammering home runs were lumbering first baseman Prince Fielder and spirited young shortstop J. J. Hardy. In 2007, Fielder, Hardy, and NL Rookie of the Year third baseman Ryan Braun energized the team. The Brewers finished 83–79. It was their first winning record since 1992. They finished in second place. But it was still not good enough for the playoffs.

SEASONS OF SUCCESS

Milwaukee's long playoff drought finally ended in 2008. Ace pitcher CC Sabathia gave the team a boost. He was acquired in a midseason trade. Sabathia went 11–2 with a 1.65 earned run average (ERA) in 17 starts with Milwaukee. The Brewers qualified for the playoffs as a Wild Card team. Their return to postseason baseball did not last long, though. The Philadelphia Phillies topped them in the NL Division Series (NLDS).

The Brewers returned to the playoffs in 2011. They were division champions for the first time since 1982. Braun was named NL MVP. He hit 33 home runs and drove in 111 runs. Fielder smacked 38 home runs and drove in 120 runs.

Third baseman Ryan Braun

EXTRA INNINGS

PRINCE FIELDER
FIRST BASEMAN
BREWERS SEASONS: 2005–11
HEIGHT: 5-FOOT-11
WEIGHT: 275 POUNDS
KEY STATS: 6X ALL-STAR, 3X SILVER SLUGGER, ALL-STAR MVP, 319 CAREER HOME RUNS

LIKE FATHER, (UN)LIKE SON

Prince Fielder was a natural slugger. His father, Cecil, had been a noted power hitter during the 1980s and '90s. Growing up, Prince spent a lot of time in his father's clubhouses. When Prince was 12, he had batting practice with Detroit coach Terry Francona. Fielder's raw power impressed Francona. "No 12-year-old should be able to hit a ball into the seats," said Francona. By coincidence, both Fielders finished their careers with 319 home runs. They are the only father and son combination to each hit at least 50 home runs in a season. One of Fielder's goals was to step out of his father's shadow. "I'm a completely different player," he explained. "One day I want people to mention my name and not have to mention his."

Milwaukee met Arizona in the NLDS. The series went to a deciding fifth game. Nyjer Morgan drove in the game-winning run with a hit in the 10th inning. The team moved on to meet St. Louis in the NL Championship Series (NLCS). The teams split the first four games. In Games 5 and 6, the Cardinals pounded Milwaukee pitchers for 19 runs. St. Louis easily won both games to win the series.

Milwaukee finished out of playoff contention for the next six seasons. In 2018, the team added versatile outfielder Christian Yelich. The move paid off. Yelich had a league-leading .326 average. He hit 36 home runs and drove in 110 runs. He was named NL MVP. Milwaukee tied with the Chicago Cubs for the division title. The Brewers won a one-game tiebreaker in Chicago to win the division.

The Brewers went on to sweep the Colorado Rockies in the NLDS. They then faced the Los Angeles Dodgers in the NLCS. The Brewers fell behind, 3-games-to-1. But they won the next two games to force a Game 7 in Milwaukee. Playing in front of the home fans did not help, though. The Dodgers won 5–1.

Milwaukee qualified for the playoffs during the next two seasons as a Wild Card team. Both appearances resulted in early playoff exits. They fell to the Washington Nationals in the NL Wild Card Game in 2019. The Brewers had a losing record in the COVID-shortened 2020 season and finished 29–31. They fell to the Dodgers in a best-of-three Wild Card Series.

Right-hander Corbin Burnes emerged as the ace of the pitching rotation in 2021. He went 11–5 with a league-leading 2.43 ERA. He was also third in strikeouts with 234. He was named the NL Cy Young Award winner. The Brewers returned to the playoffs for the fourth straight season. They won the NL Central with a 95–67 record. They faced the Atlanta Braves in the NLDS.

EXTRA INNINGS

MLB ALL-STAR GAME
JULY 9, 2002
MILLER PARK, MILWAUKEE

ALL-STAR GAME TIE

The Brewers were given the honor of hosting the 2002 MLB All-Star Game at their new home ballpark, Miller Park. The game turned out to be one of the most memorable All-Star games of all time. Minnesota Twins center fielder Torii Hunter had one of the greatest fielding plays in MLB history. He went high over the right center field fence to rob San Francisco Giants' slugger Barry Bonds of a home run. But the game was best known for ending in a tie. The score was 7–7 after 11 innings. Both teams consulted with MLB commissioner Bud Selig that the game should be stopped. There were no more pitchers available. Selig agreed to end the game. The next year a rule was enacted that gave home field advantage in the World Series to the league that won that season's All-Star game. This rule stayed through the 2016 season.

LWAUKEE

Pitcher Freddy Peralta

BREWERS
24

First baseman Rhys Hoskins

Milwaukee won the first game of the series. But Atlanta won the next three to take the series.

The Brewers won 86 games the following season. But it was not good enough for a postseason berth. Milwaukee was back in the playoffs in 2023. They won the NL Central with 92 wins. But again, they left the playoffs early. Arizona swept them in a best-of-three Wild Card Series. The Brewers won 93 games in 2024 and repeated as division champions. Outfielder Jackson Chourio emerged as a rising star. The 20-year-old batted .275 and hit 21 home runs in his rookie season. But Milwaukee fell to the New York Mets in the Wild Card Series.

The Brewers have built their history upon a simple approach. They develop talented young players into longtime fan favorites. Those fans have supported their team from the home-run happy days of the early 1980s through the disappointing seasons of the 1990s. Someday soon, the Brewers hope to hoist their first World Series trophy for their loyal fans.

Catcher William Contreras

INDEX